RUNAWAYS

RUNAWAYS

Keith Elliot Greenberg
Photographs by Carol Halebian

Lerner Publications Company / Minneapolis

Library of Congress Cataloging-in-Publication Data

Greenberg, Keith Elliot.
   Runaways / Keith Elliot Greenberg ; photographs by Carol Halebian.
       p.   cm.
     Includes bibliographical references.
     Summary: Discusses why some young people run away from troubled homes and what can happen to them and tells the stories of several teenagers who found help at Noah's Ark, a shelter run by Sister Dolores Gartanutti.
     ISBN 0-8225-2557-7 (alk. paper)
     1. Noah's Ark (Queens, New York, N.Y.)—Juvenile literature.
2. Runaway teenagers—New York (State)—Queens (New York)—Social conditions—Juvenile literature. 3. Runaway teenagers—Services for—New York (State)—Queens (New York)—Juvenile literature.
4. Homeless youth—New York (State)—Queens (New York)—Social conditions—Juvenile literature. 5. Homeless youth—Services for—New York (State)—Queens (New York)—Juvenile literature.
6. Shelters for the homeless—New York (State)—Queens (New York)—Juvenile literature. 7. Gartanutti, Dolores—Juvenile literature.
[1. Runaways. 2. Family problems. 3. Noah's Ark (Queens, New York, N.Y.) 4. Gartanutti, Dolores.] I. Halebian, Carol, ill. II. Title.
HV1437.Q44G74   1995
362.7'4—dc20   95-8074

Manufactured in the United States of America
1   2   3   4   5   6   -   JR   -   00   99   98   97   96   95

To my wife, Jennifer

The problems in Erin's home started before she was born.

The first child born to Erin's parents had died at a very young age, from pneumonia. For years afterwards, Erin's father blamed his wife for the girl's death. He said the baby became ill because his wife had kept the window open while she smoked cigarettes. Erin's mother argued that the child died not because of the open window but because the father refused to pay the electric bill.

The death of her first child sent Erin's mother into a deep depression, and she often drank heavily to try to ease her sorrow. When Erin's mother was drinking, she said nasty things to friends, neighbors, and family members. Enraged by her words, her husband often beat her.

Family pictures: Erin's parents *(top left);* mother *(top right);* the whole family—Erin, her parents, and brother *(bottom right);* and the baby who died in childhood *(bottom left).*

7

As a child, Erin remembers having to crawl on top of the washing machine to reach the phone and call the police when her father beat up her mother. Another time, Erin's father woke her up in the middle of the night and took her to a neighborhood bar. There, Erin's mother was drunkenly flirting with other men. "Look," Erin's father told her. "Look at what your mother's doing."

When Erin was nine years old, the family moved to the Rockaways, a beach area in Queens, New York. When Erin and her brother Brian tried to make friends with other kids in the neighborhood, they told Erin and Brian, "We're not allowed to play with you."

While drunk, Erin's mother had insulted the other children's parents. Erin and Brian begged their mother to apologize for the comments, but she wouldn't.

When Erin and her mother were alone, they argued so badly that sometimes they wouldn't speak to each other for two or three months afterwards. Erin's mother called her lazy and irresponsible. She predicted that her daughter would end up as a prostitute.

"When I was your age, I was baking bread," Erin's mother would say.

Erin would shoot back, "I'd love to bake bread. But you're always too drunk to teach me."

The cruelty was not limited to words. Erin's mother dumped ashtrays on her daughter and waved a knife at her while she was in bed.

Erin and her brother smiled for a picture on Easter Sunday in the Rockaways.

At age 13, Erin described in her diary how her mother often disappeared for days at a time on drinking binges. Erin wrote that the next time it happened, she hoped her mother would vanish for good.

But her mother kept coming home. Erin asked her father to save the family by getting a divorce.

He told Erin to stop making trouble—to ignore her mother.

Erin tried to spend as much time away from her family as possible. In high school, she joined the swim team and became involved in a fundraising drive for the team.

Around that time, Erin's father noticed that some money was missing from his wallet. He searched the house for it. When he discovered Erin's swim-team money, he was sure that she had stolen his money.

He took off his belt and beat his daughter with it. Erin's mother and brother ignored her screams. "I could have died and no one would have saved me," she recalled.

When the beating was over, Erin was filled with misery. She thought about killing herself. She went to the basement, got a razor blade, and prepared to slash her wrists. But she stopped at the last moment.

"I thought about the pain," she said, "and the mess I'd have to clean up if I survived."

Still, Erin knew that she could no longer live under the same roof with her family. She went upstairs, grabbed a toothbrush, and ran out the door. At age 16, Erin became a runaway.

Erin didn't run away from home because she was "bad." Although runaways have a reputation for being irresponsible, they usually have good reasons for taking the drastic step of leaving their families. Most children would prefer to live with their parents. But in situations like Erin's—when home life has become unbearable—some young people believe they have no choice but to flee.

According to the National Network of Runaway and Youth Services, between 500,000 and 1 million youth run away each year. It's impossible to determine the exact number of children living on their own, however. Some parents don't even report missing children.

Historically, runaways have been perceived as troublemakers who deserved to be disciplined. In 1977 Congress passed the Runaway Homeless Youth Act, making it illegal to arrest a child simply because he or she had run away from home. Before that time, runaways were sent to correctional facilities for juvenile offenders, even though they had committed no crime. Children who'd been battered and molested in their homes were then forced to live behind bars, while their abusive parents went unpunished.

Over the years, runaways have been given many labels, most of them negative. Runaways were called truants, delinquents, and incorrigibles. Social workers now refer to runaways in ways that reflect their situations, using terms such as homeless youth, street youth, system youth, and throwaway youth.

A study by the National Network of Runaway and Youth Services showed that 47 percent of runaways were male and 53 percent female; 54 percent were between the ages of 15 and 17, and 38 percent were under 14; 65 percent were white, 20 percent African American, 10 percent Latino, and 5 percent other ethnic groups.

In larger cities, minorities are more likely to suffer the effects of poverty, drugs, and abuse. In New York City, the majority of runaways are African American and Hispanic. Recently, a new wave of runaways includes the children of immigrants from Southeast Asia—Vietnam, Cambodia, and Laos.

Some social service agencies estimate that 20 to 40 percent of runaway and homeless youth are gay and may have been rejected by friends and family.

Regardless of a person's background, running away is usually evidence of a bad family situation. "Families are in trouble," says Margo Hirsch, executive director of the Empire State Coalition of Youth and Family Services in New York. "And the young people are the ones who are punished."

Many homeless, runaway, and street youth end up in New York City. The Times Square area is known for its sex business, and some teenage prostitutes work there.

Some common reasons children and adolescents give for running away include: physical or sexual abuse, parents in jail or on drugs, and extreme family conflict. Children who run away might feel that they couldn't relate to their parents, or that the discipline at home was unpredictable. For example, a young person was beaten for not drying the dishes properly, then was allowed to stay out all weekend.

Interestingly, few runaways drift farther than ten miles from home. Although their family relationships may be strained, these young people often want to maintain connections with friends. "Kids run away from home," Hirsch observes, "not a community."

With no place to go home to, runaways try to make the best of the situation. But it isn't easy. Some adults who offer to help have sinister motives. A man may invite a girl into his home because he wants to have sex with her. A pimp offers a young man shelter, then slowly talks him into becoming a prostitute.

Young people who leave home are at risk for a variety of dangers. One federal survey found that 20 percent of all runaway youth abused alcohol or drugs. An examination of street youth in San Francisco and New York City showed that the majority of them used at least two drugs, including alcohol.

An even greater threat is AIDS. Because runaways are likely to exchange sex for food or money, or to use intravenous drugs, they are at high risk of becoming infected with HIV, the virus that causes AIDS. One survey found that five percent of teenage runaways in New York City were infected, and eight percent in San Francisco.

The difficulty of living away from home also leads some runaways to commit suicide.

The problems of runaways can affect society in many ways. For example, when a runaway gives birth, she automatically brings a homeless person into the world. If the girl is dependent on drugs or alcohol, the baby may be born addicted. Even in the best of circumstances, a teenage mother faces more difficulties than an older, more financially secure woman. A study of 93 Los Angeles street youth between the ages of 13 and 17 found that almost half of the females had been pregnant at least once.

Vicky grew up in a tough housing project close to Erin's neighborhood in the Rockaways, Queens. Her parents were divorced, and her mother relied on welfare to make ends meet. Vicky's aunt, uncle, and cousins struggled with drug problems. But Vicky was happy because there were no drugs in her home. She and her mother liked to spend time at the beach and in the park or go shopping together. They bought matching rings and wore them.

Because they lived in a dangerous area, Vicky's mother warned her, "Don't do drugs. Stay in school. Never let guys take you away from your studies."

When Vicky was 15, she got a job in a local grocery store, making sandwiches, stocking shelves, and ringing up sales. She'd made new friends during her freshman year at Beach Channel High School, and she was spending less time at home. After a while, she noticed that her mother was acting different than she had before.

"I'd wake up in the middle of the night and I'd see my mother still awake, sitting in the living room or kitchen with this look in her eyes like she was in space," Vicky recalls. "She started asking me for money, saying she wanted to visit relatives or go shopping. Then I woke up one time and I saw people in the house, bad people, people I'd seen in the neighborhood and my mother herself had told me to stay away from."

Things got worse. When one of Vicky's gold rings disappeared, her mother accused Vicky's three-year-old brother of taking it. Vicky knew this was not true—the boy was too little to reach the top of her dresser.

"I started to think that my mother must be taking drugs," she remembers. "Her sister did it, her brother did it, my cousins did it. I hate to say it was normal, but it was part of our family."

Vicky worked up the strength to confront her mother. "You have to get help," Vicky told her. "You have a three-year-old son who needs you, and you have me."

"I'm not doing any drugs," her mother replied. "You're only 15. You shouldn't be telling me what to do. I'm your mother."

But Vicky knew what her mother was doing. Some mornings, after a night of using drugs, the woman would sober up and realize she was hurting her family. She'd approach Vicky, hug her, and apologize.

The good feelings didn't last. When Vicky received her paycheck from the grocery store, her mother asked for money. At night Vicky slept with all her jewelry on, to make sure it didn't disappear.

That fall Vicky left for school each morning with tears in her eyes. All the nighttime activity in her apartment was keeping her awake, and she started falling asleep in class. Her grades dropped from a B average the year before to a C average.

She was also tired in other ways. "I was tired of seeing my mother get high, tired of seeing those people in my house, tired of my mother leaving my little brother alone in the apartment and keeping him up all night long."

On two occasions, Vicky stormed out of the apartment in the middle of the night. "This is an area you shouldn't be walking around in the daytime," she says. "It's even worse at night." She walked past the local drug dealers and a vacant lot. With nowhere else to go, she went to the grocery store. It was closed. She sat down in front and cried.

She didn't know what to do.

"For a lot of kids like me, it's either live in the street or stay in a terrible situation," Vicky says. "If your mother's on drugs and you don't feel safe in your own house, what's the difference?"

A typical runaway finds few alternatives for shelter. One possibility is that the runaway stays with a friend or relative, who alerts the runaway's family. Then, despite the family conflict, the runaway returns home. After initially staying with friends or relatives, the runaway might overstay his or her welcome. The friends don't want a permanent guest in their home. Unwilling to return to the family, the runaway could choose to go to a shelter for homeless people.

Or, seeing no alternative, the runaway might sleep in a park, abandoned building, or in the street. The runaway may turn to crime to obtain spending money, or try to numb his or her pain with alcohol or drugs. Some runaways resort to prostitution as a way to earn money.

Even when runaways find decent shelter, they often have a hard time trusting anyone. After a lifetime of distress, they expect something bad to occur—just as it always has before.

For two decades, Sister Dolores Gartanutti has been making young people feel safe at her runaway shelter, Noah's Ark. In the 1970s, she was teaching and coaching basketball at a Catholic girl's school in Queens. Sister Dolores noticed that families were breaking down, through divorce or because of a parent's drug use. She worried that kids were falling through the cracks.

In 1977 she met a girl whose fights with her parents were so bad that she refused to go home. Sister Dolores tried to find shelter for her. "I didn't want her living on the streets," the nun remembers.

After 16 telephone calls, Sister Dolores still hadn't found a place for the young woman to stay. She realized that this wasn't an isolated case. There were many children with no place to go. And government agencies usually stepped in only after a runaway committed a crime or became addicted to drugs or alcohol. Sister Dolores decided that she wanted to help runaways before they got into trouble. She went to the other nuns in her order and announced her plan to open a shelter for runaways.

"They said it was okay, but they didn't really think I'd follow through with it," Sister Dolores says.

She quickly proved she could do it. One of the girls she coached had an uncle in the real estate business. He soon located an apartment that he let Sister Dolores use. By the next day, two young people were already living there.

Sister Dolores had grown up in a close-knit Italian-American family, and she wanted the runaways to experience something like the warmth she'd known as a child. Her parents were so impressed with her mission that they gave her the money for a down payment on a house in the Ozone Park neighborhood of Queens.

The runaways Sister Dolores took in told her tale after tale, each more horrible than the next. She wondered how they had managed to remain at home as long as they had.

"You have families where a single mother has had five children with five different men and abuses drugs, or an alcoholic father beats his wife and children, or a parent with emotional problems makes one child the scapegoat," Sister Dolores says. "No one would want to stay in these situations."

One girl whose parents were divorced was shuttled between the two of them every few weeks. "She didn't belong anywhere," Sister Dolores says. "She was like a yo-yo. Imagine feeling like no place was home."

Another girl had been flown from Ecuador to act as a servant for her aunt in Queens. The child wasn't even given a bed—she slept on the floor. When the young woman arrived at Noah's Ark, her legs were covered with bug bites.

The nun came to respect the young people for managing to survive under terrible conditions. Most of the runaways she encountered "were smart enough to leave when they did," she says. "They simply refused to settle for homes full of drugs and alcohol, and physical and sexual abuse."

In nearly two decades of running the shelter, Sister Dolores estimates that only two percent of the children she's met "were bratty and just ran away because they couldn't get their way at home." Most of them had good reasons for leaving.

Many runaways show signs of distress before they actually leave home. Sister Dolores notes, "When a kid doesn't feel wanted, it shows. They misbehave in school and cut classes."

Guidance counselors and police in Sister Dolores's area know about the shelter and have sent many young people there. The nun also visits schools, telling students about Noah's Ark.

Sister Dolores prepares a meal for the Noah's Ark residents.

At some shelters, children are beaten up and robbed by other residents as an "initiation." By contrast, the atmosphere at Noah's Ark is welcoming. "It's a family environment," Sister Dolores says. "We eat group meals. There are no locks. We share." The list of rules is short and simple: don't hurt anyone; help clean the house; obey the curfew.

Still, entering Noah's Ark for the first time can be scary. The runaways have nothing but the clothes on their backs, Sister Dolores observes. "They've left everything behind."

A Noah's Ark resident writes a letter to a friend.

As soon as a runaway arrives at Noah's Ark, Sister Dolores calls the parents to let them know where the child is. Next, the runaway is asked if he or she wants to continue attending the same school. "I encourage it, even if it's a long commute," the sister says. "They have teachers, counselors, and friends there they already trust." If the student does want to change schools, Sister Dolores arranges for registration at a local school.

Everyone seems to fit in at the small, comfortable home. Most of the runaways at Noah's Ark are female. Some are the children of doctors and lawyers. Others grew up in homeless shelters and government-run hotels for the poor. The young people are of different races and religions.

"It's been a beautiful experience," Sister Dolores says, "watching children of all colors enjoy each other, celebrate each other's holidays, share their ethnic foods. It broadens all of us."

But for all the good at Noah's Ark, the runaways still face the challenge of untangling a lifetime of negative experiences. Many of them were constantly told that they were stupid. Over time they began to believe the words, and they stopped studying or even going to school.

Sister Dolores arranges tutoring for runaways who have fallen behind in their studies. She tells the young people that it's important to get in the habit of attending school. A large number of the adolescents who've passed through Noah's Ark have gone on to college or trade school and successful adult lives.

Sister Dolores explains, "My aim is to make sure these kids have the skills to stand on their own two feet."

She also tries to bring out people's abilities. She enrolls musically gifted students in music lessons. One girl who'd been abused at home was registered for martial arts classes. For the first time in her life, she had a way to express the fury she felt in a healthy way.

On weekends and school vacations, Sister Dolores takes shelter residents to Broadway shows and on ski trips, horseback riding excursions, and trips to other cities. "It's very important to show them that there's a life away from the streets," she says.

The shelter routine on school days is almost always the same. The residents wake up, make their own breakfasts, and take turns using the bathroom. After school they do homework, watch television, visit with friends, or participate in extracurricular activities. At 5:30 P.M., everyone gathers for dinner. Sister Dolores cooks and the others clean. Then the residents are free to do whatever they please until the 11 P.M. curfew.

"If they want to stay in their rooms and read after 11, that's okay," the nun says, "as long as they're considerate and don't disturb anybody else."

As in any living situation, sometimes people feel dissatisfied. One person may think she's doing more cleaning than the others; someone else might be disturbed about the amount of noise another resident makes. Sister Dolores encourages the kids to talk about these feelings in special house meetings, held after dinner.

Occasionally a resident may suddenly fly into a rage. "They've been carrying around a lot of anger for a long time," Sister Dolores observes. "When they come here, they're grateful at first. But then, when they're comfortable, they start to feel the anger."

These difficult-to-handle feelings can lead to arguments, outrageous demands, or disruptive behavior. Some children who've experienced only turmoil feel uneasy in an environment where everything is in order. As a result, they might do things like leave the kitchen cluttered, come in late for curfew, cut classes, or use drugs or alcohol.

If a resident abuses drugs, Sister Dolores sends her to counseling. Those who simply break the house rules lose privileges such as going out on weekends. By and large, peer pressure at Noah's Ark works in a positive way: most of the residents like the shelter's atmosphere and influence the others to cooperate.

"These are basically good kids," Sister Dolores says. "When they're in a nice situation—where they're supported and loved—they make it. . . . All the talk about runaways being 'bad' isn't true, [and] their problems were never really *their* fault to begin with."

Sister Dolores and Erin

Erin had always heard that runaways became prostitutes. After leaving her house, she wondered if that would be her fate. "I wasn't sure if I could actually do that," she says. "But what else could a runaway do for money?"

For the moment, she wasn't ready to take such a drastic step. She continued to attend school, and at night she slept in a friend's garage.

After three days, she realized she couldn't stay in the garage forever. Fearful of ending up on the streets, she went to the police with her friend. Erin told the officers that she was afraid her parents would beat her to death if she returned home.

Sensing Erin's sincerity, the police reacted kindly. The officers knew Sister Dolores, and they directed Erin to Noah's Ark.

Erin's first impression of the shelter was the smell of food cooking. It made her feel welcome, like she was entering a "real home." But she was nervous that the nun would be too strict. That worry vanished as soon as she saw Sister Dolores rushing around the house with wild gray hair, using the same slang as Erin's friends.

"I thought, 'Wow, she's pretty cool,'" Erin remembers.

When Sister Dolores called in a city social worker to deal with Erin's case, the girl became worried again—maybe the city would return her to her parents. But after the social worker left, Sister Dolores calmed Erin down. "I understand why you ran away," the nun said. "You suffered abuse and neglect." It was the first time anyone had ever told Erin that her *parents* were the ones with the problem, not her.

Erin met other girls at the shelter who had been through even worse experiences. One had had her hair shaved off by her grandmother. Another was so jittery that she could not stay with the rest of the group. She sat alone for hours, nervously knitting.

This behavior didn't alarm Erin. She understood that, like her, the other girls had led difficult lives. They all found different ways to deal with their pasts, and Erin tried to be accepting of everyone.

Although her room at the house was tiny—just a bunk bed and dresser shared with another girl—Erin felt truly happy. She continued to attend her high school, commuting an hour each way on the subway, and she got a part-time job as a waitress.

Erin wasn't sure if she wanted to go to college. She'd always been told she wasn't smart enough. But Sister Dolores convinced her that she was as intelligent as anyone else. She helped her apply to colleges and arranged for the girl to receive financial aid.

Erin started classes at Potsdam College, near the New York state border with Canada. Eventually she graduated with degrees in sociology and psychology.

Erin happily celebrated her graduation from college with Sister Dolores, who helped motivate Erin to achieve her goals.

During breaks from school, Erin returned "home" to Noah's Ark. But she also stayed in touch with her real family. Maintaining any sort of relationship with them was not easy. When Erin accompanied her parents to her brother's graduation from the marines, her mother got drunk and refused to get in the car to return to New York. Erin's father left her mother behind.

As a college student, Erin was granted an internship at the New York State Legislature in Albany. The friends she met there had grown up in homes where they'd been encouraged to succeed—a very different environment from Erin's. To her amazement, though, no one shunned her because of her background.

"I fit right in," she said. "It just took me a little longer to believe in myself like they did."

Erin decided she wanted to help others like herself. She went to graduate school at Fordham University in the Bronx, earning a master's degree in social work. Now she's a social worker at Noah's Ark.

"It's so important to be able to stare someone in the face and say, 'I know what you're going through because I've been through it myself,'" she says. "I tell the kids that they've done nothing wrong—they were just raised under unfortunate circumstances. And I always let them know that they can make it, too, as long as they can see their way out of their problems."

Erin now works with children as a social worker.

One of the runaways Erin counseled was Vicky. Vicky found her way to Noah's Ark after she realized she could no longer live with a drug-addicted mother. Vicky learned about Noah's Ark when she joined a support group at school for students with parents who abused drugs.

After Vicky moved to Noah's Ark, in November 1991, the city assigned a caseworker to investigate her family. Strangely, the man reported that everything seemed normal. He recommended that Vicky return home. Vicky was shocked, and she refused to leave Noah's Ark.

"The TV's gone!" she shouted. "The furniture's gone! If you were living in that situation, where your mother's selling things one by one, there's no way you'd go back. And if you take me back [home], I'll leave again."

Vicky's mother called her at Noah's Ark and told her, "If the city takes your little brother away from me, it'll be your fault!"

"Go ahead and blame me," Vicky said. "But you caused this, not me."

After five months of arguments, her mother telephoned one day to say that she was checking herself into a drug rehabilitation program. Vicky's brother was placed in the custody of his father. It took a year for Vicky's mother to complete drug treatment, but now she is drug-free and Vicky is back home.

"It was hard for me to see the truth, that I was a drug addict," her mother told Vicky. "It was because of *you* that I got help."

Vicky and her mother are back to being friends.

Vicky was lucky. Her mother admitted her mistakes, and she changed. Some runaways never get that kind of satisfaction from their families. But if they get help—if they find someone to talk to, such as a teacher or counselor—they can avoid the dangers of the streets.

Erin comments, "Runaways are just kids who need love, somebody to believe in them and go through the bumps with them. They need someone to listen to their problems, see their talents, and say, 'You can be something remarkable.'"

Resources

Hotline Numbers

Covenant House Nineline
  (800) 999-9999 (24 hours a day,
    7 days a week)
  346 W. 17th Street, 2nd Floor
  New York, NY 10011

National Runaway Switchboard
  (800) 621-4000
  3080 N. Lincoln
  Chicago, IL 60657

Operation Home Free (a service
    provided for runaways)
  (214) 789-7200
  Greyhound/Trailways, Inc.
  15110 N. Dallas Parkway
  Dallas, TX 75248

Project Safe Place
  (502) 635-5233
  YMCA Center for Youth
    Alternatives
  1410 First Street
  Louisville, KY 40208

For More Information

Advocates for Youth
  (202) 347-5700
  1025 Vermont Avenue NW,
    Suite 200
  Washington, D.C. 20005

American Youth Work Center
  (202) 785-0764
  1200 17th St. NW, 4th Floor
  Washington, D.C. 20036

National Network of Runaway
    Youth Services
  (202) 783-7949
  1319 F Street NW, Suite 401
  Washington, D.C. 20004

National Resource Center for Youth
    Services
  (918) 585-2986
  The University of Oklahoma
    National Resource Center
  202 W. Eighth
  Tulsa, OK 74119

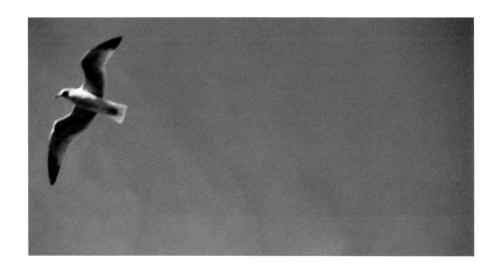

For Further Reading

Artenstein, Jeffrey. *Runaways: In Their Own Words: Kids Talking About Living on the Streets.* New York: Tor Books, 1990.

Connors, Patricia. *Runaways: Coping at Home and on the Street.* New York: Rosen Pub. Group, 1989.

Cutler, Evan Karl. *Runaway Me: A Survivor's Story.* Fort Collins, CO: A Blooming Press, 1994.

Guernsey, JoAnn Bren. *Missing Children.* New York: Crestwood House, 1990.

Landau, Elaine. *On the Streets: The Lives of Adolescent Prostitutes.* New York: Simon and Schuster, 1987.

Stavsky, Lois, and I. E. Mozeson. *The Place I Call Home: Faces and Voices of Homeless Teens.* New York: Shapolsky Pub., 1990.

Switzer, Ellen. *Anyplace But Here: Young, Alone, and Homeless: What to Do.* New York: Atheneum, 1992.